Arduino and Rasp̄[...] jarvis themed Speaking Alarm Clock, Character Recognition Tesseract, Controlling LED with Push Button, DC Motor Speed etc,..

Arduino and Rasperry Pi - Jarvis themed Speaking Alarm Clock, Character Recognition Tesseract, Controlling LED with Push Button, DC Motor Speed etc,..

CONTENTS

Acknowledgments   5

Introduction   6

1. DC Motor Control utilizing Arduino   8

2. 7 Segment Display Interfacing with Arduino   19

3. How to Use ADC in Arduino Uno?   32

4. Interfacing 16x2 LCD with Arduino   42

5. IR Controlled DC Motor utilizing Arduino   50

6. DC Motor Speed Control utilizing Arduino and   57
Potentiometer

7. Single RGB LED interfacing with Arduino Uno   66

8. Beginning with Arduino Uno: Controlling LED   74
with Push Button

9. Optical Character Recognition utilizing   97
Tesseract on Raspberry Pi

10. Raspberry Pi Based Jarvis themed Speaking   113
Alarm Clock

ACKNOWLEDGMENTS

The writer might want to recognize the diligent work of the article group in assembling this book. He might likewise want to recognize the diligent work of the Raspberry Pi Foundation and the Arduino bunch for assembling items and networks that help to make the Internet of Things increasingly open to the overall population. Yahoo for the democratization of innovation!

INTRODUCTION

The Internet of Things (IOT) is a perplexing idea comprised of numerous PCs and numerous correspondence ways. Some IOT gadgets are associated with the Internet and some are most certainly not. Some IOT gadgets structure swarms that convey among themselves. Some are intended for a solitary reason, while some are increasingly universally useful PCs. This book is intended to demonstrate to you the IOT from the back to front. By structure IOT gadgets, the per user will comprehend the essential ideas and will almost certainly develop utilizing the rudiments to make his or her very own IOT applications. These included ventures will tell the per user the best way to assemble their very own IOT ventures and to develop the models appeared. The significance of Computer Security in IOT gadgets is additionally talked about and different systems for protecting the IOT from unapproved clients or programmers. The most significant takeaway from this book is in structure the tasks yourself.

1. DC MOTOR CONTROL UTILIZING ARDUINO

Here we are going to interface a DC engine to Arduino UNO and its speed is controlled. This is finished by Pulse Width Modulation. This element is empowered in UNO to get variable voltage over steady voltage. The technique for PWM is clarified here; think about a basic circuit as shown in figure.

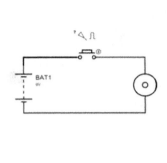

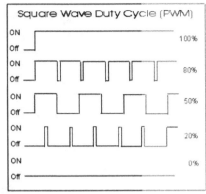

In the event that the catch is squeezed on the off chance that the figure, at that point the engine will turn over pivoting and it will be moving until the catch is squeezed. This squeezing is ceaseless and is spoken to in the primary flood of figure. On the off chance that, for a case, consider button is squeezed for 8ms and opened for 2ms over a cycle of 10ms, during this case the engine won't encounter the total 9V battery voltage as the catch is squeezed distinctly for 8ms, so the RMS terminal voltage over the engine will be around 7V. Because of this decreased RMS voltage the engine will pivot yet at a diminished speed. Presently the normal turn on over a time of 10ms = Turn ON schedule/ (Turn ON time + Turn OFF time), this is called obligation cycle and is of 80% (8/(8+2)).

In second and third cases the catch is squeezed much lesser time contrasted with first case. Along these lines, the RMS terminal voltage at the engine terminals gets even diminished further. Because of this diminished voltage the engine speed even diminishes further. This reduction in speed with obligation cycle constant to occur until a point, where the engine terminal voltage won't be adequate to turn the engine.

So by this we can finish up the PWM can be utilized to shift the engine speed.

Before going further we have to examine the H-BRIDGE. Presently this circuit has predominantly two capacities, first is to drive a DC engine from low power control signals and the other is to alter the course of revolution of DC engine.

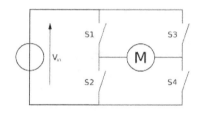

Figure 1

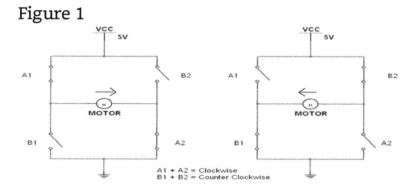

A1 + A2 = Clockwise
B1 + B2 = Counter Clockwise

Figure 2

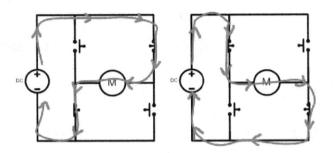

We as a whole realize that for a DC engine, to alter the course of turn, we have to change the polarities of supply voltage of engine. So to change the polarities we use H-connect. Presently in above figure1 we have fours switches. As appeared in figure2, for the engine to pivot A1 and A2 are shut. Along these lines, current courses through the engine from right to left, as appeared in second piece of figure3. Now consider the engine turns clockwise heading. Presently if the switches A1 and A2 are opened, B1 and B2 are shut. The current through the engine streams from left to directly as appeared in first piece of figure3. This course of current stream is inverse to the first thus we see a contrary potential at engine terminal to the first, so the engine pivots hostile to clock shrewd. This is the way a H-BRIDGE works. Anyway low power engines can be driven by a H-BRIDGE IC L293D.

L293D is a H-BRIDGE IC intended for driving low power DC engines and is appeared in figure. This IC comprises two h-connects thus it can drive 2 DC engines. So this IC can be utilized to drive robot's engines from the sign of microcontroller.

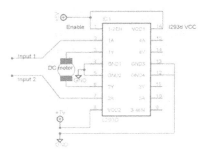

Presently as talked about before this IC has capacity to alter the course of pivot of DC engine. This is accomplished by controlling the voltage levels at INPUT 1 as well as INPUT 2.

Enable Pin	Input Pin 1	Input Pin 2	Motor Direction
High	Low	High	Turn Right
High	High	Low	Turn Left
High	Low	Low	Stop
High	High	High	Stop

So as appeared in above figure, for clockwise turn 2A ought to be high and 1A ought to be low. Also for against clockwise 1A ought to be high and 2A ought to be low.

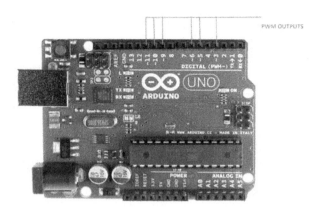

As appeared in the figure, Arduino UNO has 6 Pulse Width Modulation channels, so we can get PWM (variable voltage) at any of these six pins. In this instructional exercise we are gonna to utilize PIN3 as PWM yield.

Equipment: ARDUINO UNO, control supply (5v), 100uF capacitor ,LED, catches (two pieces), 10K? resistor (two pieces).

Programming: arduino IDE (Arduino daily).
Circuit Diagram

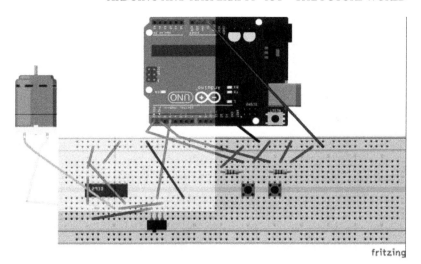

fritzing

The circuit is associated in breadboard according to the circuit graph appeared previously. Anyway one must focus during associating the LED terminals. Despite the fact that the catches show skipping impact for this situation it doesn't cause significant blunders so we need not stress this time.

The PWM from UNO is simple, on typical events setting up an ATMEGA controller for PWM signal isn't simple, we need to characterize numerous registers and settings for an exact sign, anyway in ARDUINO we don't need to manage each one of those things.

As a matter of course all the header records and registers are predefined by ARDUINO IDE, we basically need to call them and that is it we will have a PWM yield at fitting pin.

Presently for getting a PWM yield at a proper stick, we

have to take a shot at three things,

1. pinMode(ledPin, OUTPUT)
2. analogWrite(pin, value)
3. analogWriteResolution(neededresolutionnumber)

First we have to pick the PWM yield stick from six pins, after that we have to set that stick as yield.

Next we have to empower the PWM highlight of UNO by calling the capacity "analogWrite(pin, esteem)". In here 'stick' speak to the stick number where we need PWM yield we are putting it as '3'. So at PIN3 we are getting PWM yield.

Worth is the turn ON obligation cycle, between 0 (constantly off) and 255 (consistently on). We are going to addition and decrement this number by button press.

The UNO has a most extreme goals of "8", one can't go further henceforth the qualities from 0-255. Anyway one can diminish the goals of PWM by utilizing order "analogWriteResolution()", by entering an incentive from 4-8 in the sections, we can change its incentive from four piece PWM to eight piece PWM.

The switch is to alter the course of pivot for DC engine.

Code

```
volatile int i=0;//initializing a integer for in-
crementing and decrementing duty ratio.
void setup()
{
        pinMode(3, OUTPUT);   // sets the pin3
as output
        pinMode(0, INPUT);// sets the pin0 as
output
        pinMode(1, INPUT);// sets the pin1 as
output
}
void loop()
{
        analogWrite(3, i); // analogWrite values
from 0 to 255
        if (digitalRead(0)==LOW)
        {
                if (i<255)
                {
                        i++;//if pin0 is pressed
and the duty ratio value is less than 255
                        delay(30);
                }
        }
```

```
            if (digitalRead(1)==LOW)
        {
                if (i>0)
                {
                        i--;// if pin1 is pressed
and the duty ratio value is greater than 0
                        delay(30);
                }
        }
}
```

◆ ◆ ◆

2. 7 SEGMENT DISPLAY INTERFACING WITH ARDUINO

In this instructional exercise we are gonna to interface a 7 portion show to ARDUINO UNO. The showcase checks from 0-9 and resets itself to zero. Prior to going further, let us initially examine around seven section shows.

A seven section show got its name from the very truth that it got seven lighting up portions. Every one of these portions has a LED (Light Emitting Diode), thus the lighting. The LEDs are created to such an extent that lighting of each LED is contained to its very own section. The significant thing to see here that the LEDs in any seven section show are masterminded in like manner anode mode (normal positive) or basic cathode mode (regular negative).

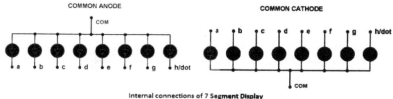

Internal connections of 7 Segment Display

The circuit association of LEDs in like manner cathode and regular anode is appeared in above figure. Here one can see that, in CC the -ve terminals of each LED is associated together as well as brought out as GND. In CA the positive of each LED is associated together and brought out as VCC. These CC and CA come in extremely helpful while multiplexing a few cells together.

Components Required

Equipment: ARDUINO UNO , control supply (5v), HDSP5503 seven portion show (two pieces) (any normal cathode will do), 47uF capacitor (associated crosswise over power supply).

Programming: arduino IDE (Arduino daily)
Circuit Diagram and Working Explanation

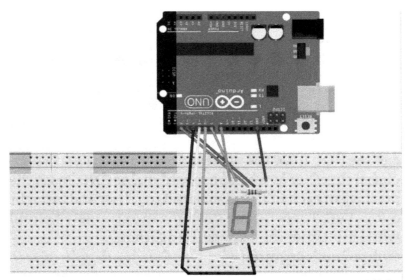

fritzing

The associations which are accomplished for 7 fragment show are given underneath:

PIN1 otherwise E to PIN 6 of ARDUINO UNO

PIN2 otherwise D to PIN 5

PIN4 otherwise C to PIN 4

PIN5 otherwise H otherwise DP to PIN 9/not required as we are not utilizing decimal point

PIN6 otherwise B to PIN 3

PIN7 otherwise A to PIN 2

PIN9 otherwise F to PIN 7

PIN10 otherwise G to PIN 8

PIN3 otherwise PIN8 otherwise CC to ground through 100? resistor.

Presently to comprehend the working, consider a seven section show is associated with a port, so state we have associated "A fragment of show to PIN0", "B portion of show to PIN1", "A portion of show to PIN3", "A fragment of show to PIN4", "A section of show to PIN5", "A portion of show to PIN6". Furthermore, is shared conviction type as appeared in figure.

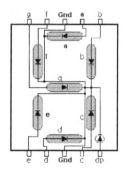

Here the shared conviction must be associated with ground for the showcase to work. One can check each fragment of show by utilizing multimeter in diode mode. Each section ought not be control with a voltage more noteworthy than 4v, whenever did the presentation will be harmed forever. For maintaining a strategic distance from this a typical resistor can be supplier at regular terminal, as appeared in circuit chart.

Presently, in case we need to show a "0" in this presentation as appeared in beneath figure.

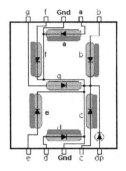

We have to turn the LEDs of portions "A, B, C, D, E F", so we have to control PIN0, PIN1, PIN2, PIN3, PIN4 and PIN5. So every time we require a "0", we have to control every one of the pins referenced.

Presently, on the off chance that we need "1" in plain view

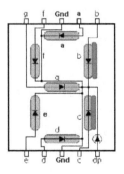

We have to control fragments "B, C", for portion B, C to turn ON we have to control PIN1, PIN2. With both the pins high we get "1" in plain view. So as observed above we are going to control pins comparing to the digit that to be appeared in plain view.

Here we will compose a program killing each portion ON and for a check 0-9. The working of 0-9 counter is best clarified bit by bit in C code given underneath:

Code

```
#define segA 2//connecting segment A to PIN2
#define segB 3// connecting segment B to PIN3
#define segC 4// connecting segment C to PIN4
#define segD 5// connecting segment D to PIN5
#define segE 6// connecting segment E to PIN6
#define segF 7// connecting segment F to PIN7
#define segG 8// connecting segment G to PIN8
        int COUNT=0;//count integer for 0-9 increment
void setup()
{
        for (int i=2;i<9;i++)
        {
```

```
            pinMode(i, OUTPUT);// taking
all pins from 2-8 as output
        }
}
void loop()
{
switch (COUNT)
        {
            case 0://when count value is zero
show"0" on disp
        digitalWrite(segA, HIGH);
        digitalWrite(segB, HIGH);
        digitalWrite(segC, HIGH);
        digitalWrite(segD, HIGH);
        digitalWrite(segE, HIGH);
        digitalWrite(segF, HIGH);
        digitalWrite(segG, LOW);
        break;
            case 1:// when count value is 1 show"1"
on disp
        digitalWrite(segA, LOW);
        digitalWrite(segB, HIGH);
        digitalWrite(segC, HIGH);
        digitalWrite(segD, LOW);
```

```
digitalWrite(segE, LOW);
digitalWrite(segF, LOW);
digitalWrite(segG, LOW);
break;
case 2:// when count value is 2 show"2"
on disp
digitalWrite(segA, HIGH);
digitalWrite(segB, HIGH);
digitalWrite(segC, LOW);
digitalWrite(segD, HIGH);
digitalWrite(segE, HIGH);
digitalWrite(segF, LOW);
digitalWrite(segG, HIGH);
break;
case 3:// when count value is 3 show"3"
on disp
digitalWrite(segA, HIGH);
digitalWrite(segB, HIGH);
digitalWrite(segC, HIGH);
digitalWrite(segD, HIGH);
digitalWrite(segE, LOW);
digitalWrite(segF, LOW);
digitalWrite(segG, HIGH);
break;
```

```
        case 4://when count value is 4 show"4"
on disp
            digitalWrite(segA, LOW);
            digitalWrite(segB, HIGH);
            digitalWrite(segC, HIGH);
            digitalWrite(segD, LOW);
            digitalWrite(segE, LOW);
            digitalWrite(segF, HIGH);
            digitalWrite(segG, HIGH);
            break;
        case 5://when count value is 5 show"5"
on disp
            digitalWrite(segA, HIGH);
            digitalWrite(segB, LOW);
            digitalWrite(segC, HIGH);
            digitalWrite(segD, HIGH);
            digitalWrite(segE, LOW);
            digitalWrite(segF, HIGH);
            digitalWrite(segG, HIGH);
            break;
        case 6://when count value is 6 show"6"
on disp
            digitalWrite(segA, HIGH);
            digitalWrite(segB, LOW);
```

```
digitalWrite(segC, HIGH);
digitalWrite(segD, HIGH);
digitalWrite(segE, HIGH);
digitalWrite(segF, HIGH);
digitalWrite(segG, HIGH);
break;
case 7:// when count value is 7 show"7"
on disp
digitalWrite(segA, HIGH);
digitalWrite(segB, HIGH);
digitalWrite(segC, HIGH);
digitalWrite(segD, LOW);
digitalWrite(segE, LOW);
digitalWrite(segF, LOW);
digitalWrite(segG, LOW);
break;
case 8:// when count value is 8 show"8"
on disp
digitalWrite(segA, HIGH);
digitalWrite(segB, HIGH);
digitalWrite(segC, HIGH);
digitalWrite(segD, HIGH);
digitalWrite(segE, HIGH);
digitalWrite(segF, HIGH);
```

```
        digitalWrite(segG, HIGH);
        break;
    case 9:// when count value is 9 show"9"
on disp
        digitalWrite(segA, HIGH);
        digitalWrite(segB, HIGH);
        digitalWrite(segC, HIGH);
        digitalWrite(segD, HIGH);
        digitalWrite(segE, LOW);
        digitalWrite(segF, HIGH);
        digitalWrite(segG, HIGH);
        break;
        break;
    }
    if (COUNT<10)
    {
            COUNT++;
            delay(1000);///increment count
integer for every second
    }
    if (COUNT==10)
    {
            COUNT=0;// if count integer
value is equal to 10, reset it to zero.
```

```
        delay(1000);
    }
}
```

❖ ❖ ❖

3. HOW TO USE ADC IN ARDUINO UNO?

In this instructional exercise we are presenting idea of Analog to Digital Conversion in ARDUINO UNO. Arduino board has 6 Analog to Digital Conversion channels, as show in fig underneath. Among those any one or every one of them can be utilized as contributions for simple voltage. The Arduino Uno ADC is of 10 piece goals (so the whole number qualities from (0-(2^10) 1023)). This implies it will delineate voltages somewhere in the range of 0 and 5 volts into whole number qualities somewhere in the range of 0 and 1023. So for each (5/1024 = 4.9mV) / unit.

In the entirety of this we will interface a potentiometer or pot to the 'A0' channel, and we are gonna to show the ADC result on a straightforward showcase. The basic presentations are 16x1 and 16x2 showcase units. The 16x1 presentation unit will have 16 characters and are in one line. The 16x2 will have 32 characters altogether 16in first line and another 16 in second line. Here one must comprehend that in each character there are 5x10=50 pixels so to show one character every one of the 50 pixels must cooperate, yet we need not need to stress over that in light in case there an another controller (HD44780) in the showcase unit which carries out the responsibility of controlling the pixels (you can see it in LCD unit, it is the bruised eye at the back).

Components Required

Equipment: ARDUINO UNO, control supply (5v), 100uF capacitor, JHD_162ALCD (16x2LCD), 100nF capacitor, 100K? pot otherwise potentiometer.

Programming: arduino IDE (Arduino daily)

Circuit Diagram and Explanation

In 16x2 LCD there are 16 sticks over all if there is a backdrop illumination, if there is no backdrop illumination there will be 14 pins. One can power or leave the backdrop illumination pins. Presently in the 14 pins there are 8 information pins (7-14 otherwise D0-D7), 2 power supply pins (1&2 otherwise VSS&VDD otherwise GND&+5v), third stick for differentiate control (VEE-controls how thick the characters ought to be appeared), as well as 3 control pins (RS&RW&E).

In the circuit, you can watch I have just took two control sticks, the differentiation bit and READ/WRITE are not regularly utilized so they can be shorted to ground. This places LCD in most noteworthy complexity and read mode. We simply require to control ENABLE and RS pins to send characters and information in like manner.

The associations which are accomplished for LCD are given underneath:

PIN1 otherwise VSS to ground

PIN2 otherwise VDD or VCC to +5v control

PIN3 otherwise VEE to ground (gives most extreme difference best for a learner)

PIN4 otherwise (Register Selection) to PIN8 of ARDUINO UNO

PIN5 otherwise (Read/Write) to ground (places LCD in read mode facilitates the correspondence for client)

PIN6 otherwise (Enable) to PIN9 of ARDUINO UNO

PIN11 otherwise D4 to PIN10 of ARDUINO UNO

PIN12 otherwise D5 to PIN11 of ARDUINO UNO

PIN13 otherwise D6 to PIN12 of ARDUINO UNO

PIN14 otherwise D7 to PIN13 of ARDUINO UNO

The ARDUINO IDE enables the client to utilize LCD in 4 piece mode. This kind of correspondence empowers the client to diminish the stick utilization on ARDUINO, not at all like other the ARDUINO need not be modified independently for utilizing it in 4 it mode on the grounds that of course the ARDUINO is set up to convey in 4 piece mode. In the circuit you can view we utilized 4bit correspondence (D4-D7).

So from insignificant perception from above table we are interfacing 6 pins of LCD to controller in which 4 pins are information pins and 2 pins for control.

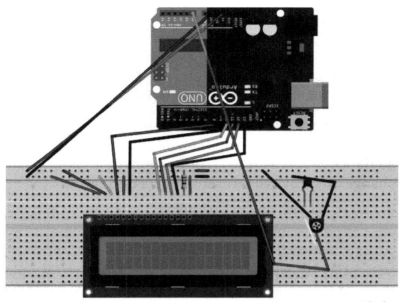

fritzing

The above fig shows the circuit graph of Analog to Digital Conversion of ARDUINO UNO.
Working

For interfacing a LCD to the ARDUINO UNO, we have to know a couple of things.

1. analogRead(pin);
2. analogReference();
3. analogReadResolution(bits);

Most importantly the UNO ADC channels has a default reference estimation of 5V. This implies we can give a greatest information voltage of 5V for ADC transformation at any information channel. Since certain sensors give voltages from 0-2.5V, with a 5V reference we get lesser precision, so we have a guidance that empowers us to change this reference esteem. So for changing the reference esteem we have ("analogReference();")

As default we get the most extreme board ADC goals which is 10bits, this goals can be changed by utilizing guidance ("analogReadResolution(bits);"). This goals change can prove to be useful for certain cases.

Presently if the above conditions are set to default, we can peruse an incentive from ADC of channel '0' by straightforwardly calling capacity "analogRead(pin);", here "stick" speaks to stick where we associated simple sign, for this situation it would be "A0". The incentive from ADC can be taken into a whole number as "int AD-CVALUE = analogRead(A0); ", by this guidance the incentive after ADC gets put away in the whole number "ADCVALUE".

Presently how about we talk somewhat about 16x2 LCD. First we have to empower the header record ('#include <LiquidCrystal.h>'), this header document has guidelines written in it, which empowers the client to interface a LCD to UNO in 4 piece mode with no fluff. With this header document we need not need to send information to LCD a tiny bit at a time, this will all be dealt with as well as we don't require to compose a program for sending information or an order to LCD a little at a time.

Second we have to tell the board which kind of LCD we

are utilizing here. Since we have such a significant number of various sorts of LCD (like 20x4, 16x2, 16x1 and so forth.). Here we are gonna to interface a 16x2 LCD to the UNO so we get 'lcd.begin(16, 2);'. For 16x1 we get 'lcd.begin(16, 1);'.

In this guidance we are gonna to tell the board where we associated the pins, The pins which are associated are to be spoken to all together as "RS, En, D4, D5, D6, D7". These pins are to be spoken to accurately. Since we associated RS to PIN0, etc as show in circuit chart, We speak to the stick number to board as "LiquidCrystal lcd(0, 1, 8, 9, 10, 11);".

After above there all there is left is to send information, the information which should be shown in LCD ought to be composed as " cd.print("hello, world!");". With this order the LCD shows 'hi, world!'.

As should be obvious we need not stress over any this else, we simply need to introduce and the UNO will be prepared to show information. We don't need to compose a program circle to send the information BYTE by BYTE here.

Utilizing ADC of Arduino Uno is clarified bit by bit in C program given underneath.

Code

```
#include <LiquidCrystal.h>
// initialize the library with the numbers of the
```

interface pins

```
LiquidCrystal lcd(8, 9, 10, 11, 12, 13); // REGIS-
TER SELECT PIN,ENABLE PIN,D4 PIN,D5 PIN,
D6 PIN, D7 PIN
char ADCSHOW[5]; //initializing a character of
size 5 for showing the ADC result
void setup()
{
// set up the LCD's number of columns and
rows:
lcd.begin(16, 2);
}
void loop()
{
// set the cursor to column 0, line 1
lcd.print("  HELLO WORLD"); //print name
lcd.setCursor(0, 1); // set the cursor to column
0, line
lcd.print("ADC RESULT:"); //print name
String       ADCVALUE      =      String(analo-
gRead(A0)); //intailizing a string and storing
ADC value in it
ADCVALUE.toCharArray(ADCSHOW,  5);  //
convert the reading to a char array
lcd.print(ADCSHOW); //showing character of
```

ADCSHOW

```
lcd.print("  ");
lcd.setCursor(0, 0); // set the cursor to column
0, line1
}
```

◆ ◆ ◆

4. INTERFACING 16X2 LCD WITH ARDUINO

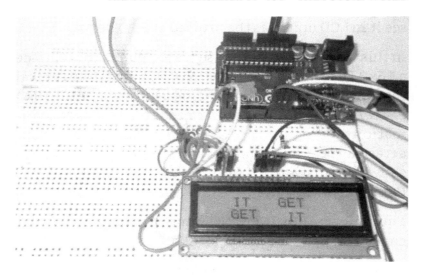

To set up a decent correspondence between human world and machine world, show units assume a significant job. Thus they are a significant piece of implanted frameworks. Show units - enormous or little, chip away at a similar essential standard. Other than complex show units like realistic presentations and 3D dispays, one must know working with basic shows like 16x1 and 16x2 units. The 16x1 showcase unit will have 16 characters as well as are in 1 line. The 16x2 LCD will have 32 characters altogether 16in first line as well as another 16 in second line. Here one must comprehend that in each character there are 5x10=50 pixels so to show one character every one of the 50 pixels must cooperate. In any case, we need not to stress over that in light of the fact that there is another controller (HD44780) in the presentation unit which carries out the responsibility of controlling the pixels. (you can see it in LCD unit, it is the bruised eye at the back).

In this instructional exercise we are gonna to interface a 16x2 LCD with ARDUINO UNO. Not at all like typical improvement sheets interfacing a LCD to an ARDUINO is very simple. Here we don't need to stress over information sending and accepting. We simply need to characterize the stick numbers and it will be prepared to show information on LCD.

Components Required

Equipment: ARDUINO UNO, control supply (5v), 100uF capacitor, JHD_162ALCD(16x2LCD).

Programming: Arduino IDE (Arduino daily).

Circuit Diagram and Explanation

In 16x2 LCD there are 16 sticks over all if there is a backdrop illumination, if there is no backdrop illumination there will be 14 pins. One can power or leave the backdrop illumination pins. Presently in the 14 pins there are 8 information pins (7-14 otherwise D0-D7), 2 power supply pins (1&2 otherwise VSS&VDD otherwise GND&+5v), third stick for differentiate control (VEE-controls how thick the characters ought to be appeared), as well as 3 control pins (RS&RW&E).

In the circuit, you can watch I have just took two control sticks, this gives the adaptability. The complexity bit and READ/WRITE are not frequently utilized so they can be shorted to ground. This places LCD in most elevated difference and read mode. We simply require to control ENABLE as well as RS pins to send characters as well as information in like manner.

The associations which are accomplished for LCD are given underneath:

PIN1 otherwise VSS to ground

PIN2 otherwise VDD otherwise VCC to +5v control

PIN3 otherwise VEE to ground (gives most extreme differentiation best for a learner)

PIN4 otherwise (Register Selection) to PIN0 of AR-DUINO UNO

PIN5 otherwise (Read/Write) to ground (places LCD in read mode facilitates the correspondence for client)

PIN6 otherwise (Enable) to PIN1 of ARDUINO UNO

PIN11 otherwise D4 to PIN8 of ARDUINO UNO

PIN12 otherwise D5 to PIN9 of ARDUINO UNO

PIN13 otherwise D6 to PIN10 of ARDUINO UNO

PIN14 otherwise D7 to PIN11 of ARDUINO UNO

The ARDUINO IDE enables the client to utilize LCD in 4 piece mode. This sort of correspondence empowers the client to diminish the stick utilization on ARDUINO, not at all like other the ARDUINO need not to be customized independently for utilizing it in 4 it mode in light of the fact that of course the ARDUINO is set up to convey in 4 piece mode. In the circuit you can see we have utilized 4bit correspondence (D4-D7).

So from minor perception from above table we are associating 6 pins of LCD to controller in which 4 pins are information pins and 2 pins for control.

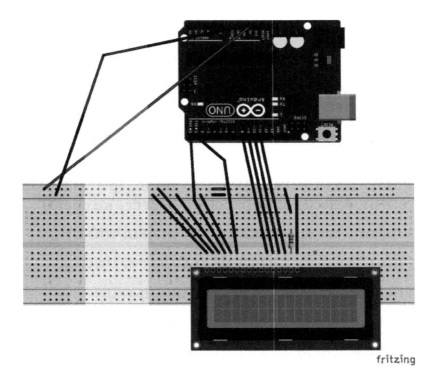

fritzing

The above figure shows the circuit chart of 16x2 LCD associated with ARDUINO UNO.

Working

To interface a LCD to the ARDUINO UNO, we have to know a couple of things.

1. #include <LiquidCrystal.h>
2. lcd.begin(16, 2);

3. LiquidCrystal lcd(0, 1, 8, 9, 10, 11);
4. lcd.print("hello, world!");

As by the above table we just require to take a gander at these four lines for setting up a correspondence between an ARDUINO and LCD.

First we have to empower the header document ('#include <LiquidCrystal.h>'), this header record has directions written in it, which empowers the client to interface a LCD to UNO in 4 piece mode with no fluff. With this header document we need not need to send information to LCD a little bit at a time, this will all be dealt with as well as we don't require to compose a program for sending information or a direction to LCD a tiny bit at a time.

Second we have to tell the board which sort of LCD we are utilizing here. Since we have such a significant number of various sorts of LCD (like 20x4, 16x2, 16x1 and so on.). Here we are gonna to interface a 16x2 LCD to the UNO so we get 'lcd.begin(16, 2);'. For 16x1 we get 'lcd.begin(16, 1);'.

In this guidance we are going to tell the board where we associated the pins. The pins which are associated should be spoken to all together as "RS, En, D4, D5, D6, D7". These pins are to be spoken to accurately. Since we have associated RS to PIN0, etc as show in the circuit graph, we speak to the stick number to board as "LiquidCrystal lcd(0, 1, 8, 9, 10, 11);". The information which should be shown in LCD ought to be composed as " cd.print("hello, world!");". With this order the LCD shows 'hi, world!'.

As should be obvious we need not to stress over whatever else, we simply need to instate and the UNO will be prepared to show information. We don't require to compose a program circle to send the information BYTE by BYTE here.

The method for correspondence among LCD and UNO is clarified bit by bit in C code given beneath:

Code

```
#include <LiquidCrystal.h>
// initialize the library with the numbers of the interface pins
LiquidCrystal lcd(0, 1, 8, 9, 10, 11); /// REGISTER SELECT PIN,ENABLE PIN,D4 PIN,D5 PIN, D6 PIN, D7 PIN
void setup()
{
    // set up the LCD's number of columns and rows:
lcd.begin(16, 2);
}
void loop()
{
```

```
// set the cursor to column 0, line 1
lcd.print("  HELLO WORLD");//print name
lcd.setCursor(0, 1); // set the cursor to column
0, line 2
lcd.print("www.its_me_anbazha-
gan_k.com");//print name
delay(750);//delay of 0.75sec
lcd.scrollDisplayLeft();//shifting data on LCD
lcd.setCursor(0, 0);// set the cursor to column
0, line1
}
```

◆ ◆ ◆

5. IR CONTROLLED DC MOTOR UTILIZING ARDUINO

Arduino has become the most famous Microcontroller among understudies and specialists in less length of time. So everybody attempt to utilize Arduino to make any extend, as it is simple and having smooth expectation to learn and adapt. We have made numerous Arduino ventures from essential interfacing activities to cutting edge automated tasks and IoT ventures, you can check every one of them in our site.

Today we are making a straightforward task with Arduino which utilizes three fundamental segments that are IR Sensor, Relay Module and DC Motor. Here we will interface Infrared sensor with Arduino to control Direct-Current Motor. Here IR sensor will recognize any article before it and Arduino will peruse the IR Sensor's yield and make the Relay High. Hand-off is additionally

associated with DC Motor, so DC Motor will be ON at whatever point IR Sensor Detects any items in front it.
Required Components:

- Arduino UNO
- 5V-relay module
- DC motor
- IR sensor module
- Breadboard
- Connecting wires

Relay Module

DC Motor

IR Sensor Module

Circuit Diagram and Explanation:

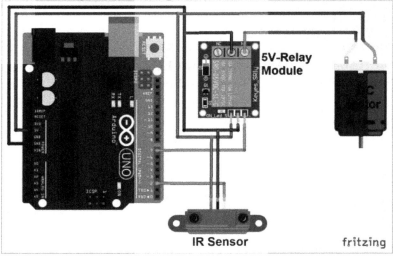

Circuit of this IR Sensor controlled DC Motor with Arduino is basic as demonstrated as follows:

In circuit, IR sensor Module yield stick is basic combined with the Pin 2 no of Arduino and Relay Module's info is combined with Pin 7 no of Arduino. Further a DC Motor is associated with the Relay.

To study IR Sensor, Relay and DC Motor, you can experience following activities:

- IR Sensor Module Circuit

- Arduino Relay Control Tutorial

- DC Motor Control utilizing Arduino

Code Explanation:

Code for this task is straightforward. Complete Arduino Code is given toward the end.

Here we have associated IR sensor yield stick to Pin 2 of Arduino. So at whatever point IR sensor recognizes any articles Pin 2 of Arduino will be high and dependent on that Relay will be turned on which is combined with Pin 7 of Arduino.

```
void setup() {

pinMode(2,INPUT);

pinMode(7,OUTPUT);

Serial.begin(9600);

}

void loop() {

  if (digitalRead(2) == 1)
```

```
{

  Serial.println(digitalRead(2));

  digitalWrite(7,HIGH);

}
```

Working of IR controlled DC Motor with Arduino:

Working of this task is straight forward. At whatever point there is some item before IR sensor, it will distinguish that and make the yield stick high. IR sensor's yield stick is associated with Arduino, so Arduino will understand it and actuate the Relay module by making pin 7 high. When transfer is enacted, it will turn on the DC engine.

When there is no item close to IR sensor, the yield of IR sensor will stay low and DC engine will likewise stay in Off state. The affectability of IR Sensor can be balanced using the potentiometer on the module itself. Affectability basically implies the good ways from which it can recognize the article.

Code
```
void setup() {
pinMode(2,INPUT);
pinMode(7,OUTPUT);
```

```
Serial.begin(9600);
}
void loop() {
  if (digitalRead(2) == 1)
{
  Serial.println(digitalRead(2));
  digitalWrite(7,HIGH);
}
else{
  digitalWrite(7,LOW);
  }
}
```

❖ ❖ ❖

6. DC MOTOR SPEED CONTROL UTILIZING ARDUINO AND POTENTIOMETER

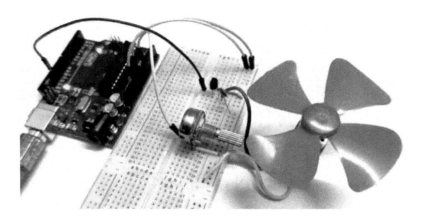

DC engine is the most utilized engine in Robotics and gadgets ventures. For managing the speed of DC engine we have different strategies, however in this task we are controlling DC Motor speed utilizing PWM. In this task we will have the option to control the speed of DC engine with potentiometer and we can alter the speed by turning the handle of Potentiometer.

Pulse Width Modulation:

What is Pulse Width Modulation? Pulse Width Modulation is a strategy by utilizing we can manage the voltage or power. To comprehend it all the more basically, in the event that you are applying 5 volt for driving an engine, at that point engine will moving with some speed, presently on the off chance that we diminishes applied voltage by 2 methods we apply 3 volt to engine at that point engine speed likewise diminishes. This idea is utilized in the venture to control the voltage utilizing PWM. (To see progressively about PWM, check this circuit: 1 Watt LED Dimmer)

% Duty cycle = (TON/(TON + TOFF)) *100

Where, T_{ON} = HIGH time of the square wave

T_{OFF} = LOW time of square wave

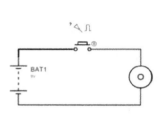

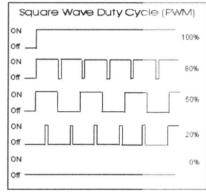

Presently if the switch in the figure is shut consistently over some undefined time frame then the engine will persistently ON during that time. On the off chance that the switch is shut for 8ms and opened for 2ms over a cycle of 10ms, at that point the Motor will be ON just during the 8ms time. Presently the normal terminal over the over a time of 10ms = Turn ON schedule/ (Turn ON time + Turn OFF time), this is called obligation cycle and is of 80% (8/(8+2)), so the normal yield voltage will be 80% of the battery voltage. Presently human eye can't see that engine is on for 8ms and off for

2ms, so will look like DC Motor is pivoting with 80% speed.

In the subsequent case, the switch is shut for 5ms and opened for 5ms over a time of 10ms, so the normal terminal voltage at the yield will be half of the battery voltage. State if the battery voltage is 5V and the obligation cycle is half thus the normal terminal voltage will be 2.5V.

In the third case the obligation cycle is 20% and the normal terminal voltage is 20% of the battery voltage.

We have utilized PWM with Arduino in a considerable lot of our Projects:

- Arduino Based LED Dimmer utilizing PWM
- Temperature Controlled Fan utilizing Arduino
- DC Motor Control utilizing Arduino

Material Required
- Arduino UNO
- DC motor
- Transistor 2N2222
- Potentiometer 100k ohm
- Capacitor 0.1uF
- Breadboard
- Jumping Wires

Circuit Diagram

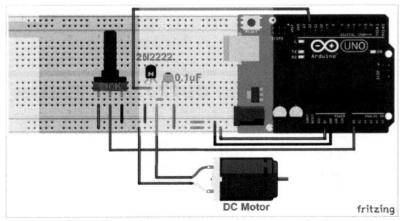

DC Motor   fritzing

Code and Explanation

The total Arduino code for controlling DC engine speed utilizing potentiometer is given toward the end.

In the underneath code, we have introduced the variable c1 and c2 and relegated simple stick A0 for the potentiometer yield and twelfth Pin for 'pwm'.

```
int pwmPin = 12;

int pot = A0;

int c1 = 0;

int c2 = 0;
```

Presently, in the underneath code, setting pin A0 as info and 12 (which is PWM stick) as yield.

```
void setup() {

  pinMode(pwmPin, OUTPUT); // declares
  pin 12 as output

  pinMode(pot, INPUT);  // declares pin A0
  as input

}
```

Presently, in void circle (), we are perusing the simple worth (from A0) utilizing analogRead(pot), and sparing it to variable c2. At that point, subtract c2 esteem from 1024 and spare the outcome in c1. At that point make the PWM stick twelfth of Arduino HIGH and afterward after a deferral of significant worth c1 make that stick LOW. Once more, after a deferral of significant worth c2 the circle proceeds.

The explanation behind subtracting Analog incentive from 1024 is, the Arduino Uno ADC is of 10-piece goals (so the whole number qualities from $0 - 2^{10}$ = 1024 qualities). This implies it will delineate voltages somewhere in the range of 0 and 5 volts into number qualities somewhere in the range of 0 and 1024. So in case we duplicate information anlogValue to (5/1024), at that point we get the computerized estimation of information voltage. Learn here how to utilize ADC contribution to Arduino.

```
void loop()

{

  c2 = analogRead(pot);

  c1 = 1024-c2;

  digitalWrite(pwmPin, HIGH); // sets pin
12 HIGH

  delayMicroseconds(c1);  // waits for c1 uS
(high time)

  digitalWrite(pwmPin, LOW);  // sets pin
12 LOW

  delayMicroseconds(c2);  // waits for c2 uS
(low time)

}
```

Working Explanation:

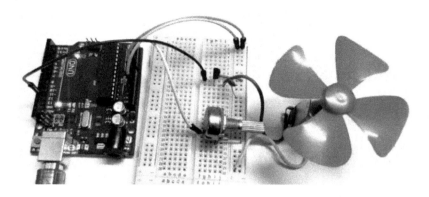

In this circuit, for controlling the speed of DC engine, we utilize a 100K ohm potentiometer to change the obligation cycle of the PWM signal. 100K ohm potentiometer is associated with the simple input stick A0 of the Arduino UNO and the DC engine is associated with the twelfth stick of the Arduino (which is the PWM stick). The working of Arduino program is basic, as it peruses the voltage from the simple stick A0. The voltage at simple stick is fluctuated by utilizing the potentiometer. Subsequent to doing some fundamental estimation the obligation cycle is balanced by it.

For instance, in the event that we feed 256 incentive to the simple information, at that point the HIGH time will be 768ms (1024-256) and LOW time will be 256ms. In this manner, it essentially implies the obligation cycle is 75%. Our eyes can't see such high recurrence swaying and it would appear that engine is constantly ON with 75% of speed. With the goal that's the manner by which we can control the speed utilizing Potentiometer.

Code

```
int pwmPin = 12; // assigns pin 12 to variable
pwm
int pot = A0; // assigns analog input A0 to vari-
able pot
int c1 = 0;  // declares variable c1
int c2 = 0;  // declares variable c2
void setup()  // setup loop
{
 pinMode(pwmPin, OUTPUT);
 pinMode(pot, INPUT);
}
void loop()
{
 c2= analogRead(pot);
 c1= 1024-c2;     // subtracts c2 from 1000 ans
saves the result in c1
 digitalWrite(pwmPin, HIGH);
 delayMicroseconds(c1);
 digitalWrite(pwmPin, LOW);
 delayMicroseconds(c2);
}
```

◆ ◆ ◆

7. SINGLE RGB LED INTERFACING WITH ARDUINO UNO

In this task we are gonna to interface (Red Green Blue) LED with Arduino Uno. A run of the mill RGB LED is appeared in underneath figure:

The RGB LED will have four sticks as appeared in figure.

- **PIN1:** Color 1 negative terminal in like manner anode or shading 1 positive terminal in like manner cathode

- **PIN2:** Common positive for every one of the three hues in Common anode type or regular negative for each of the three hues in like manner cathode type RGB LED.

- **PIN3:** Color 2 negative terminal or shading 2 positive terminal

- **PIN4:** Color 3 negative terminal or shading 3 positive terminal

So there are two sorts of RGB LEDs, one is normal cathode type (regular negative) and other is basic anode type (basic positive) type. In CC (Common Cathode or Common Negative), there will be three positive terminals every terminal speaking to a shading and one negative terminal speaking to each of the three hues. The interior circuit of a CC RGB LED can be spoken to as beneath.

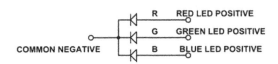

Common Cathode RGB LED

In Common Cathode type, If we need RED to be On in above, we have to control the RED LED stick and ground the regular negative. The equivalent goes for every one of the LEDs. In CA (Common Anode or Common Positive), there will be three negative terminals every terminal speaking to a shading and one positive terminal speaking to each of the three hues.

The inside circuit of a CA RGB LED can be spoken to as

appeared in figure.

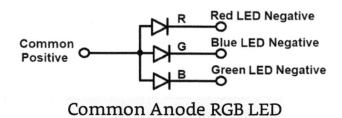

R — Red LED Negative

G — Blue LED Negative

B — Green LED Negative

Common Anode RGB LED

In Common Anode type, on the off chance that we need RED to be on in above, we have to ground the RED LED stick and power the regular positive. The equivalent goes for every one of the LEDs.

In our circuit we are going to utilize CA (Common Anode or Common Positive) type. On the off chance that you need to associate more RGB LEDs, state 5, at that point you need 5x4= 20 PINS for the most part, however we can diminish this PIN utilization to 8 by interfacing RGB LEDs in parallel and by utilizing a strategy called multiplexing.

Required Components:
- Arduino Uno
- Resistor – 1k
- Red Green Blue LED (Common Anode)

Circuit and Working Explanation

The circuit association for Red Green Blue LED Arduino interfacing is appeared in beneath figure.

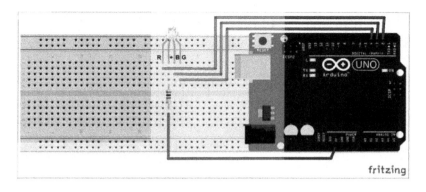

Here we have associated Common Anode terminal of RGB LED with the 5v supply of Arduino alongside a 1k Resistor.

Presently Negative pins (1, 3, 4) of RGB LED is associated with Arduino Pin 2, 3 and 4. Here RGB LED is associated backward rationale implies in the event that we make ground terminal of LED high, it will kill. So here we are making ground terminal of RGB LED high to keep the separate LED in off state. What's more, on the off chance that we make ground terminal of RGB LED low it will sparkle.

So as we have just observed in above stick chart of RGB LED that stick 2 is normal anode, and stick 1, 3 and 4 are the ground terminals of Red, blue and green shading individually.

In underneath code, you can watch that we are then again flickering each of the 3 hues in RGB drove by making the Ground terminals of RGB high and low. Recall that LED will be off when ground terminal of separate shading is high and LED will sparkle when ground Terminal of Respective shading is Low.

This is the manner by which we program a RGB LED with Arduino, in the event that you need utilize Multiple RGB LEDs with Arduino, at that point check this one.

Code

```
void setup() {

    pinMode(2, OUTPUT);

    pinMode(3, OUTPUT);

    pinMode(4, OUTPUT);

}
void loop() {
 digitalWrite(2, LOW);
 delay(500);

    digitalWrite(2, HIGH);
 delay(500);

    digitalWrite(3, LOW);
```

```
delay(500);

digitalWrite(3, HIGH);
delay(500);
digitalWrite(4, LOW);
delay(500);

digitalWrite(4, HIGH);
delay(500);
}
```

❖ ❖ ❖

8. BEGINNING WITH ARDUINO UNO: CONTROLLING LED WITH PUSH BUTTON

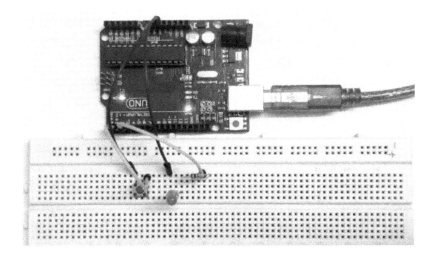

The name Arduino is regularly popular expression among the vast majority of the hardware understudies or specialists the same. Its capacity to construct things quicker and less expensive with a gigantic online network support has settled on it a perfect decision for some individuals who are simply beginning with hardware or programming. In light of its disentangled equipment plan and programming condition, it is conceivable in any event, for individuals with no gadgets or software engineering foundation to learn it easily. So what really is this Arduino? How might you begin with it? What would you be able to make with it to improve your way of life?

Every one of these inquiries will be attempted to be replied in this instructional exercise, as we step through. We will set up the Arduino IDE on your PC/Laptop and transfer an example flicker program to the Arduino. At that point we will likewise assemble a little equipment utilizing a bread board with a straightforward circuit comprising of a switch and LED and program our Arduino as indicated by it. Sounds fascinating enough?!!

What actually is Arduino?

Before we start learning Arduino, we should initially realize what it is. This is significant in light issue that there is a typical misguided judgment among individuals that Arduino is a microcontroller. This isn't valid, how about we make it unmistakable here that Arduino isn't a microcontroller. So what's going on here?

Arduino is an open-source improvement stage which comprises of a simple to utilize equipment as well as a programming situation. Here the simple to utilize equipment alludes to the Arduino UNO and the programming condition alludes to the Arduino IDE. There are numerous equipment board other than Arduino UNO like the Arduino Mega, nano, small scale and so forth.. In any case, with the end goal of this instructional exercise we will stay with just Arduino UNO. The Arduino IDE is the product utilizing which we will program the Arduino UNO board.

Setting up the Arduino IDE

The initial phase in our procedure will be to set up the Arduino IDE on your Laptop/PC. The beneath guidelines are immediate for windows clients just, for different stages the system is nearly the equivalent. On the off chance that you get some issue Mac clients and

Linux clients can utilize the particular connections. Likewise ensure you have the administrator privileges of the PC for simple establishment.

Stage 1: Download the Arduino IDE structure the

authority Arduino site, by basically tapping on the

connection beneath

https://www.arduino.cc/download_handler.php

Stage 2: This will download an exe document, which will be the most recent Arduino IDE of your time. When I am reporting this, the most recent variant is Arduino-1.8.5 and the size of the document is 90.4MB. There is an excellent possibility that it got refreshed when you are giving this a shot.

Once the download is finished dispatch the exe document. You may be requested administrator rights, whenever provoked snap on yes.

Stage 3: Click on "I Agree" to consent to the License Agreement of Arduino.

Stage 4: Next Under Installation alternatives, ensure all the checkboxes are ticked as appeared beneath and afterward click on straightaway.

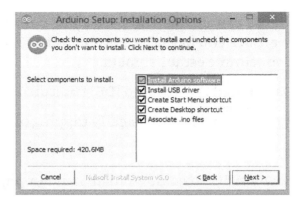

Stage 5: Now, we need to choose the area at which the IDE must be introduced. As a matter of course, it will be introduced under Program records index of C drive. It is high prescribed to leave it all things considered and click on Install

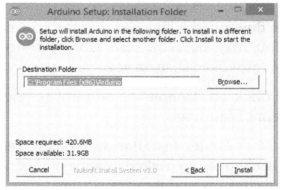

Stage 5: You should see the IDE getting introduced on your PC. Hold up till the advancement bar is completed. The screen will be something like this demonstrated as follows. When finished it will show "finished" at that point click on the nearby catch.

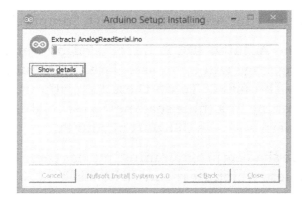

Stage 6: After shutting the installer. Go to your work area and discover the Arduino exe record and dispatch it. It will show a boot up name and afterward open the IDE with an absolute minimum code on it as demonstrated as follows

Connecting your Arduino board with Computer:

When the Arduino IDE is introduced on our PC, the following stage will be to associate the Arduino UNO board with our PC. To do these basically utilize the programming link (blue shading) to associate your Arduino board with the USB port of your PC.

This blue shading programming link has three capacity in complete which are recorded beneath

1. It gives the necessary capacity to the Arduino UNO to work, so you can run your ventures just by straightforwardly controlling them however the USB link

2. It programs the ATmega328 microcontroller on the Arduino UNO board. The program you compose on the IDE is sent into the microcontroller through this link

3. It goes about as a sequential correspondence link; it can converse with the PC through sequential correspondence going about as a decent troubleshooting device. You will see increasingly about this as we burrow profound.

When the board is controlled you will view a little LED remaining high. This is to show that the board is provided with control. You ought to likewise see another LED flickering because of the default squint program which was at that point transferred by the merchant on your Arduino UNO

Since this is the first occasion when you are interfacing your load up to the PC, it may set aside some effort for the drivers to start establishment naturally. How about we check if the board was found effectively by our PC. To do this quest for "Gadget chief" on your PC.

In the wake of opening gadget chief there will an alternative called "Ports (COM and LPT)" click on it and check if the board is recorded under that choice as demonstrated as follows

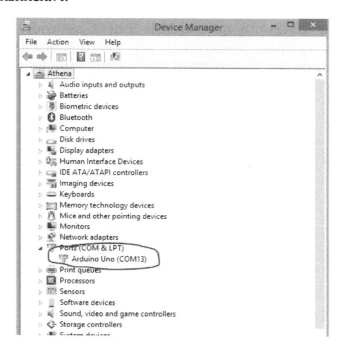

Note: The Port name for my Arduino board has showed up as Arduino Uno, the name of your Arduino may contrast dependent on the board seller. It very well may be CCH450 or something to that effect so don't stress over the name of the port.

In the event that you can't discover the choice called "Ports (COM and LPT)" it implies your board isn't found. All things considered it is a driver issue, so you need to physically introduce the right drivers for your board.

Sometimes you will discover more than one COM port recorded under the ports area and you won't know which one is for the Arduino load up since the naming will likewise be extraordinary. All things considered simply separate the board and interface once more. Check which COM port is vanishing and showing up once more, this COM port is your Arduino UNO.

When you have discovered the right COM port note down the COM port number of your board. Here for my board the COM port number is 13. This number will change each time you change the USB port to which the load up is associated with.

Uploading the blink program

Presently, we should transfer our first program to the Arduino board through the Arduino IDE that we just downloaded. The Arduino IDE when introduced accompanies some model projects which comes exceptionally convenient for tenderfoots. So we should open one of the model projects by picking File - > Examples - > Basics - > Blink as demonstrated as follows

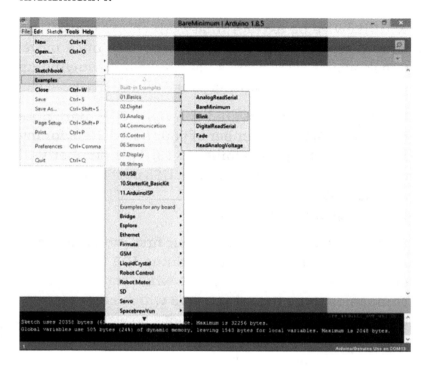

This will open the Blink program; the target of the program is to flicker the Led on the Arduino board. When the program is opened we need to choose the right board. To choose the board that we are utilizing pick Tool - > Boards - > Arduino UNO/Genuino as demonstrated as follows

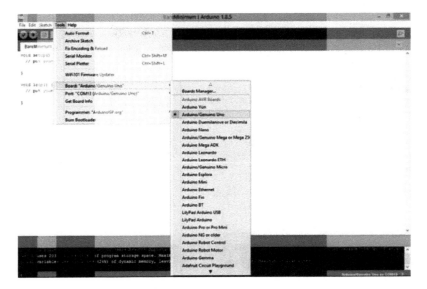

Next, we need to choose the right COM port for our board. We previously noticed that the COM port for my Arduino was COM13. It could have been distinctive for you. To choose the Com port pick Tools - > Port - > COM13

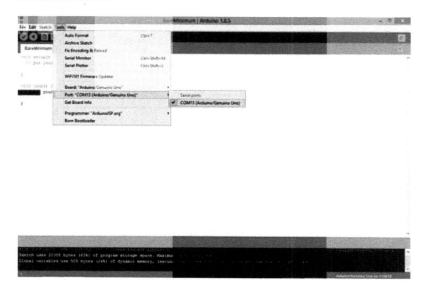

In the event that everything is right you should see Arduino UNO on COM 13 as the base of the screen. In the wake of confirming that snap on the transfer symbol (featured in Blue) to transfer the code to the Board as demonstrated as follows

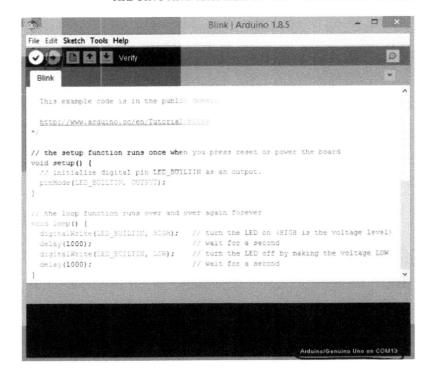

When the catch is squeezed, you will see "Aggregating portrayal" and afterward, if the code is transferred effectively you will consider a to be as "Done Uploading" as demonstrated as follows

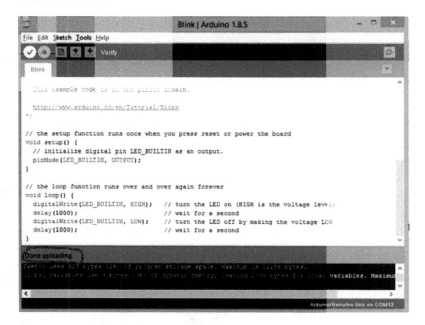

That is it we have transferred the main program to the Arduino board with progress. Be that as it may, what's going on here? What have we done? What is the yield of the program? To know the appropriate response of every one of these inquiries how about we assemble a little equipment utilizing which we can gleam a LED when a catch is squeezed and compose the program all by our self without any preparation

Materials Required:

The materials required for this venture are

- Arduino UNO
- Push Button
- Programming Cable

- 1k resistor
- LED (any color)
- Connecting wires
- Bread Board

Hardware Connection:

The total association graph of the set-up is demonstrated as follows. You simply need to pursue the figure to make the associations accordingly.

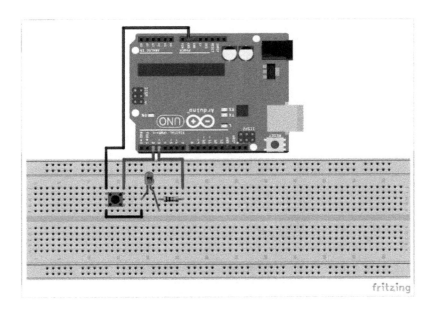

In our equipment the push button is input which is associated with the second stick of the Arduino. In case you investigate you can see that one side of the catch is associated with the Ground and the opposite side is associated with stick number 2. This implies at whatever point we press the catch the stick number 2 will be associated with ground

Next the LED is associated with stick number 3 through a resistor of 1k. Again the cathode stick of drove (the shorted stick) is associated with ground and the anode stick (longer stick) is associated with stick 3 through a resistor. This resistor is known as a present constraining resistor as it confines the measure of current coursing through the LED. In case this current isn't constrained abundance current will move through the LED harming it for all time.

Programming your Arduino:

Since our equipment is prepared we can begin programming our Arduino UNO board. The total Arduino program will be given toward the finish of this page, further beneath we are simply experiencing them line by line.

For each Arduino program there ought to be two capacities by obligatory. These two capacities are void arrangement () and void circle (), they are known as the absolute minimum. Everything that we compose inside the void arrangement () will be executed once and everything that we compose inside void circle will be execute again and again. Both the capacities are demonstrated as follows, this is the thing that you get when you select File - > New.

```
void setup() {

  // put your setup code here, to run once:

}

void loop() {

  // put your main code here, to run repeatedly:

}
```

How about we start composing program into the arrangement () work. Ordinarily the stick revelations will be done inside the arrangement() work. In our equipment we need to pronounce that stick 2 is an info stick and the stick 3 is a yield stick. This should be possible by the accompanying lines

```
pinMode(2,INPUT);

pinMode (3,OUTPUT);
```

Be that as it may, we have a little change here, since the stick 2 is utilized as INPUT it ought to never be left skimming. Which means an info stick ought to consistently be associated either to +5V or to ground. For our situation the information will be associated with ground just in the event that we press the catch and in the event that we don't press the catch it will be left drifting. To evade this we go through something many refer to as inward force resistor. This resistor is available inside the ATmega 328 microcontroller and you can't see it. To utilize this resistor we simply need to compose a line on out Arduino IDE.

This line will interface the stick number 2 +5V through a resistor subsequently making it to go high when not associated with ground. So we change the catchphrase INPUT as INPUT_PULLUP as demonstrated as follows

```
pinMode(2,INPUT_PULLUP);
```

Since we have finished with our arrangement () work, let us move to the circle () work. Here we need to check if the stick 2 is grounded (LOW) and in the event that it is grounded we need to make the LED shine by making it pin3 HIGH. If not grounded (else) we need to keep the LED killed by making the stick 3 as LOW. Give us a chance to place these words in program like

```
if (digitalRead(2) == LOW)

{

  digitalWrite(3,HIGH);

}

else

{

  digitalWrite(3,LOW);

}
```

Here the term digitalRead() is utilized to peruse the status of an INPUT stick. In case the stick is associated with ground it will return LOW and if the stick is associated with +5V it will return HIGH.

Correspondingly, the term digitalWrite() is utilized to set the status of an OUTPUT stick. In the event that we set the stick as HIGH it will give +5V as yield and in the event that we set the stick as LOW it will give 0V as yield.

So for our program, when we press the catch stick 2 will be grounded (LOW), so we make stick 3 to yield +5V (HIGH). This +5V will be sufficient to turn on the LED. On the off chance that this condition isn't met, at that point stick 3 will be made 0V (LOW) which will in the long run mood killer the LED.

That is it our program is finished, given us a chance to transfer the code to our Arduino board, much the same as how we transferred the squint code above.
Verifying our output:

When we have effectively transferred the code to the Arduino load up the time has come to confirm the yield of our program. The equipment association of my Arduino is demonstrated as follows, to confirm the yield we should simply press the push fasten and check if the LED is turning on. At that point when we discharge it the LED should kill.

In the event that you have any issue in getting this work, you can brief you issue in the remark area for help. Or again you can likewise utilize the discussions for specialized assistance. Expectation you comprehended the instructional exercise and made your first small step with Arduino, when you get settled with this essential you can jump profound to investigate Arduino considerably more.

In the wake of knowing the rudiments about the Arduino you can attempt interface the essential segments like 16x2 LCD, DC Motor, Servo Motor, Keypad and so forth.

Code

```
void setup() {
pinMode(2,INPUT_PULLUP);
pinMode (3,OUTPUT);
}
void loop() {
 // put your main code here, to run repeatedly:
 if (digitalRead(2) == LOW)
 {
  digitalWrite(3,HIGH);
 }
 else
 {
  digitalWrite(3,LOW);
 }
}
```

❖ ❖ ❖

9. OPTICAL CHARACTER RECOGNITION UTILIZING TESSERACT ON RASPBERRY PI

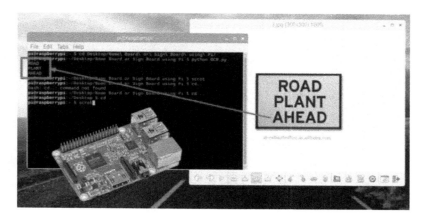

The capacity of machines to utilize a camera to take a gander at this present reality and interpret? information from it would affect its applications. Be it a basic nourishment conveyance Robot like the Starship Robots or a propelled self driving vehicle like Tesla, they are depend on data gotten from their profoundly complex cameras to take choices. In this instructional exercise we will find out how subtleties are distinguished from pictures by perusing the characters present on it. This is called Optical Character Recognition.

This opens entryway for some, applications like to consequently peruse the data from a business card, perceive a shop from its name board or perceive sign sheets on street and substantially more. A few of us may have just encountered these highlights through Google Viewpoint, so today we will fabricate something comparative utilizing an Optical Character Recognition (OCR) Tool from Google Tesseract-OCR Engine alongside python and OpenCV to personality characters from pictures with a Raspberry Pi.

Raspberry pi, being a convenient and less power expending gadget, is utilized in some ongoing picture handling applications like Face recognition, object following, Home security framework, Surveillance camera and so forth.

Pre-requisites

As told before we will utilize the OpenCV Library to distinguish and perceive faces. So make a point to introduce OpenCV Library on Raspberry Pi before continuing with this instructional exercise. Additionally Power your Pi with a 2A connector as well as combine it to a presentation screen for simpler troubleshooting.

This instructional exercise won't clarify how precisely OpenCV functions, in case you are keen on learning Image preparing, at that point look at this OpenCV nuts and bolts and propelled Image handling instructional exercises. You can figure out about shapes, Blob Detection and so on in this Image Segmentation instructional exercise utilizing OpenCV.

Installing Tesseract on Raspberry Pi

To perform OCR on Raspberry Pi, we need to introduce the Tesseract OCR motor on Pi. To do this we need to initially arrange the Debian Package (dpkg) which will assist us with installing the Tesseract OCR. Utilize the underneath order on the terminal window to design Debian Package.

sudo dpkg - -configure –a

At that point we can continue with introducing the Tesseract OCR (Optical Character Recognition) utilizing the well-suited get alternative. The direction for the equivalent is given underneath.

sudo apt-get install tesseract-ocr

Your terminal window will look like beneath, it will take around 5-10 minutes for the establishment to finish.

Since we have the Tesseract OCR introduced we need

to introduce the PyTesseract bundle utilizing the pip introduce bundle. Pytesseract is a python wrapper around the tesseract OCR motor, which causes us to utilize tesseract with python. Pursue the beneath order to introduce pytesseract on python.

Pip install pytesseract

Ensure pad is as of now introduced before you continue to this progression. Individuals who have pursued the Raspberry Pi face acknowledgment instructional exercise would have just introduced it. Other can utilize that instructional exercise and introduce it now. Once the pytesseract establishment is finished you window will look something like this

Tesseract 4.0 on Windows/Ubuntu

The Tesseract Optical character acknowledgment venture was initially begun by Hewlett Packard in 1980 and afterward was embraced by Google which keeps up the undertaking till date. Throughout the years the Tesseract has advanced, yet at the mean time it functions admirably just in controlled situations. In case the picture has an excess of foundation clamor or is out of center tesseract doesn't appear to function admirably there.

To conquer this, the most recent variant of tesseract, the Tesseract 4.0 uses a Deep Learning model to perceive characters and even penmanship styles. Tesseract 4.0 uses Long Short-Term Memory as well as Recurrent Neural Network to improve the precision of its OCR motor. Lamentably through during this season of this instructional exercise Tesseract 4.0 is accessible for Windows and Ubuntu, however is still in beta stage for the Raspberry Pi. So we chose to attempt Tesseract 4.0 on windows and Tesseract 3.04 on Raspberry Pi.
Simple Character Recognition Program on Pi

Since we have just introduced the Tesseract OCR and Pytesseract bundles in our PI. We can rapidly compose a little program to check how the character acknowledgment is functioning with a test picture. The test picture I utilized, the program and the outcome can be found in the beneath picture.

Explain
that
Stuff!
0123456789O

This is 1.png

As should be obvious the program is truly basic and we didn't utilize any OpenCV bundles. The above program is given underneath

---

from PIL import Image

img =Image.open ('1.png')

text = pytesseract.image_to_string(img, config=")

print (text)

In the above program we are attempting to peruse content from a picture called '1.png' which is situated inside a similar catalog of the program. The Pillow bundle is utilized to open this picture and spare it under the variable name img. At that point we utilize the image_to_sting strategy from the pytesseract bundle to distinguish any content from the picture and spare it as a string in the variable content. At last we print the estimation of content to check the outcomes.

As should be obvious the first picture really contains the content "Clarify that Stuff! 01234567890" which is an ideal test picture since we have letter sets, images and numbers in the picture. In any situation, the yield that we get from pi is "Clarify that stuff! Sdfiosiefoewufv" this implies out program neglects to perceive any numbers from the picture. To conquer this issue individual typically use OpenCV to expel commotion from the program and afterward arrange the Tesseract OCR motor dependent on the picture to show signs of improvement results. In any case, recollect that you can't expect 100% solid yield from Tesseract OCR Python.

Configuring the Tesseract OCR for improved results

Pytesseract enables us to arrange the Tesseract OCR motor by setting the banners which changes the manner by which the picture is scanned for characters. The three primary banners utilized in arranging a Tesseract OCR is language (-l), OCR Engine Mode (- - oem) and Page Segmentation Mode (- - psm).

Alongside the default English language, Tesseract bolsters numerous different dialects including Hindi, Turkish, French and so forth. We might be utilizing English here, however you can install the prepared information from official github page and add it up to your bundle to perceive different dialects. It is additionally conceivable to perceive at least two distinctive language from a similar picture. The language is set by banner – l, to set it to a language utilize the code alongside banner, for instance for English it will be – l eng, where eng is the code for English.

The following banner is the OCR Engine Mode, it has four unique modes. Every mode utilizes an alternate calculation to perceive the characters from the Image. Of course it utilizes the calculation that got introduced with the bundle. Be that as it may, we can transform it to utilize LSTM or Neural nets. The four diverse Engine modes is demonstrated as follows. The banner is shown by - oem, so to set it to mode 1, just use - oem 1.

```
OCR Engine modes:
  0    Legacy engine only.
  1    Neural nets LSTM engine only.
  2    Legacy + LSTM engines.
  3    Default, based on what is available.
```

The Final and the most significant banner is the page division mode banner. These are helpful when your picture has so a lot of foundation subtleties alongside the characters or the characters are written in various direction or size. There are absolutely 14 diverse page division mode, every one of them are recorded beneath. The banner is shown by – psm, so to set the method of 11. It will be – psm 11.

```
Page segmentation modes:
  0    Orientation and script detection (OSD) only.
  1    Automatic page segmentation with OSD.
  2    Automatic page segmentation, but no OSD, or OCR.
  3    Fully automatic page segmentation, but no OSD. (Default)
  4    Assume a single column of text of variable sizes.
  5    Assume a single uniform block of vertically aligned text.
  6    Assume a single uniform block of text.
  7    Treat the image as a single text line.
  8    Treat the image as a single word.
  9    Treat the image as a single word in a circle.
 10    Treat the image as a single character.
 11    Sparse text. Find as much text as possible in no particular order.
 12    Sparse text with OSD.
 13    Raw line. Treat the image as a single text line,
       bypassing hacks that are Tesseract-specific.
```

Using oem and psm in Tesseract Raspberry Pi for better results

Give us a chance to check how compelling these design modes are. In the underneath picture I have attempted to perceive the characters in a speed limit board which says "SPEED LIMIT 35". As should be obvious the number 35 is in huge size contrasted with different letter sets which confounds the Tesseract and hence we get yield just as "SPEED LIMIT" and the number is absent.

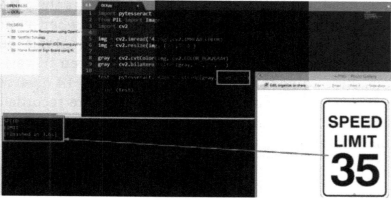

To conquer this issue, we can set the config banners.

In the above program the config banner is unfilled config=", now let us set it utilizing the subtleties gave previously. All the content in the picture is English so language banner is – l eng, the OCR motor can be left as default which is mode 3 so – oem 3. Presently at long last on the psm mode, we have to discover more characters from the picture so we utilize the mode 11 here, which becomes – psm 11. The last config line will resemble

test = pytesseract.image_to_string(gray, config='-l eng --oem 3 --psm 12')

What's more, the outcome for the equivalent can be found beneath. As should be obvious now the Tesseract can locate the every one of the characters from the picture including the numbers.

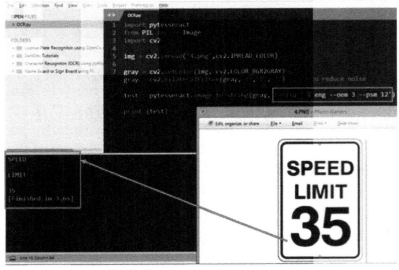

Improving accuracy with confidence level

Another fascinating element that is accessible in Tesseract is the image_to_data strategy. This strategy can give us subtleties like situation of the character in the picture, the certainty level of identification, line and page number. We should give utilizing this a shot an example picture

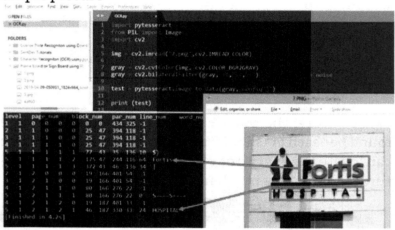

In this specific model, we get a great deal of clamor data alongside the first data. The picture is the name leading body of a medical clinic called "Fortis Hospital". In any case, alongside the name the picture additionally has other foundation subtleties like logo building and so on. So the Tesseract take a stab at changing over everything into content and gives us a great deal of commotion like "$C" "|" "S_____S==+" and so forth.

Presently in these cases the image_to_data strategy proves to be useful. As should be obvious here, the above optical character acknowledgment calculation restores the certainty level of each character that it has perceived and the certainty level of Fortis is 64 and for HOSPITAL it is 24. For the other loud data the certainty esteem is 10 or beneath than 10. In this way we can sift through the helpful data and improve the precision utilizing the estimation of certainty.

OCR on Raspberry PI

Despite the fact that the outcomes are not fulfilling on Pi when utilizing Tesseract, it tends to be joined with OpenCV to sift through clamor from picture and other design strategy can be utilized to get not too bad outcomes if the photos are great. We have just attempted around 7 distinct pictures with tesseract on Pi and were bundle to get close outcomes by tweaking the modes as needs be for each image. The total undertaking document can be installed as Zip for this area, which has all the test pictures and the essential code.

How about we attempt one more example load up sign on Raspberry Pi, this time one which is exceptionally plain and straightforward. The code for the equivalent is given underneath.

```
import pytesseract

from PIL import Image

import cv2
```

```
img = cv2.imread('4.png',cv2.IMREAD_
COLOR) #Open the image from which cha-
rectors has to be recognized

#img = cv2.resize(img, (620,480) ) #resize
the image if required

gray = cv2.cvtColor(img, cv2.COLOR_B-
GR2GRAY) #convert to grey to reduce de-
tials

gray = cv2.bilateralFilter(gray, 11, 17, 17)
#Blur to reduce noise

original = pytesseract.image_to_string(g-
ray, config=")

#test = (pytesseract.image_to_data(gray,
lang=None, config=", nice=0) ) #get confi-
dence level if required

#print(pytesseract.image_to_boxes(gray))

print (original)
```

The program opens the record from which we have
to perceive the characters from and afterward changes

over it to grayscale. This will decrease the subtleties from the picture making it simpler for Tesseract to perceive characters. Further to decrease the foundation commotion we obscure the picture utilizing a respective channel which is a technique from OpenCV. At long last we start perceiving characters from the picture and print it on the screen. The conclusive outcome will be something like this.

Expectation you comprehended the instructional exercise and delighted in gaining some new useful knowledge. OCR is utilized in numerous spots such as self driving vehicles, License plate acknowledgment, road board acknowledgment route and so forth and utilizing it on Raspberry Pi opens entryway to part more conceivable outcomes since it tends to be convenient and smaller. Additionally check our other Image Processing based activities here.

Complete python code for this OCR content acknowledgment is given beneath, it very well may be additionally downloaded from here with every one of the pictures to test the program.

◆ ◆ ◆

10. RASPBERRY PI BASED JARVIS THEMED SPEAKING ALARM CLOCK

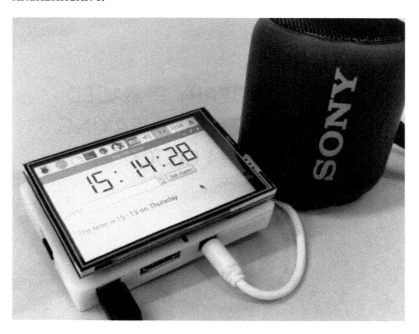

"Hello. It's 7:00 a.m. The climate in Malibu is 72 degrees with dissipated mists. The surf conditions are reasonable with midsection to-bear high lines. Elevated tide will be at 10:52 a.m". Each time I hear this voice of Jarvis in the motion picture Iron Man it sends me chills down my spine. I am certain simply like me many would have longed for carrying on with a real existence as refined as Tony Stark. In any case, unfortunately we have not progressed with innovation for a small scale Arc reactor or an AI as savvy as

JARVIS. Be that as it may, it is conceivable to supplant our exhausting morning timers with the one that is like Jarvis utilizing a Raspberry Pi. Toward the finish of this venture, we will make an extremely fundamental GUI utilizing which we can set an alert and when the caution goes on we will have a voice which reveals to us the present time and day with some pre-characterized content. Sounds cool right!! So let us assemble one.

Materials Needed

- Raspberry Pi
- 3.5" TFT LCD Screen
- Speaker
- AUX cable
- Internet Connection

Pre-Requisites

It is accepted that your Raspberry Pi is as of now flashed with a working framework and can interface with the web. If not, pursue the Getting started with Raspberry Pi instructional exercise before continuing. Here we are utilizing Rasbian Jessie introduced Raspberry Pi 3.

It is likewise accepted that you approach your pi either through terminal windows or through other application utilizing which you can compose and execute python projects and utilize the terminal window.

You may likewise need to look at how to interface 3.5" TFT LCD with Raspberry Pi since we will utilize it in this undertaking.
Install TTS Engine (Espeak) for Raspberry Pi

As the task title states we are going to construct a talking clock. So as to cause your Pi to talk we need a Text To discourse (TTS) Engine. There are large number of choices to choose from, however for straightforwardness I have select the Espeak Engine. To introduce Espeak on your Pi essentially run the accompanying direction on your terminal

```
sudo apt-get install espeak

sudo apt-get install espeak python-espeak
```

Creating GUI for Raspberry Pi Speaking Alarm Clock

For this undertaking we have to build up a GUI that speaks to a morning timer with the goal that the client can view the present time and furthermore set the caution. There are loads of alternatives to build up a GUI utilizing Python, yet the most mainstream and flexible one is the PyQt4, so we will utilize that to build up our GUI. In the beneath hardly any headings we talk about how to utilize PyQt4 to structure your own GUI's, however on the off chance that you are not intrigued you can legitimately avoid down to "Program for Speaking Alarm Clock" heading.

Introducing PyQt4 with Qt fashioner on your Windows Machine

Since we are structuring a GUI we will initially begin our programming on our PC (windows/Linux) and afterward port this python content to chip away at our Pi. Since PyQt4 has an excellent transportability most engineers do this since the advancement is simple and quicker in a PC at that point really doing it on a Raspberry Pi.

I have introduced python and PQt bundles on my windows machine; on the off chance that you are not keen on this you can build up your GUI on your raspberry pi itself by essentially skirting this progression. To introduce PQt on windows download this exe document and during the establishment system ensure you have checked the Qt creator programming since we will utilize it for our task.

Introducing PyQt on Pi/Linux/MAC machines

To introduce PyQt on Linux machine just run the accompanying line on your direction terminal

sudo apt-get install python-qt4

Designing the GUI using Qt Designer

One recognizable favorable position of utilizing PyQt4 for your GUI plans is that it has

Qt planner programming. This product can be utilized to make button, presentations, writings and different illustrations by essentially hauling things into screen and setting them any place required. This spares us a huge deal of time since we don't need to physically bolster in the estimate and position of the articles on our screen. I have introduced Qt fashioner alongside Python and PyQt4 on my windows PC utilizing the exe record as talked about in above passage. In the wake of introducing open your Qt Designer as well as you will get this screen.

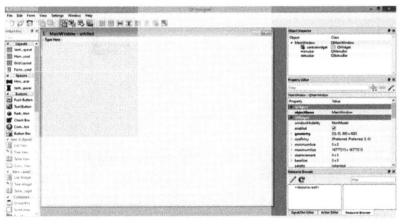

On the left side you can discover design, spacers, catches and different things which you can essentially use by hauling it into your window. You can likewise tweak the items as required utilizing the windows on the right. I have utilized a 7-section LCD show, a catch, a book line and set time item to make the UI for our morning timer. In the wake of utilizing formats to put every items in the necessary place and size my window looked something like this underneath

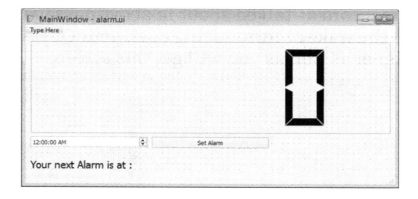

When your GUI is prepared you can spare your structure as a .ui record. Afterward, whenever you wish to cause changes to your GUI you to can basically open this document and do the progressions without looking here and there in your program. The .ui document for talking clock can be downloaded on the off chance that you wish to roll out any improvements to this structure. When you are happy with the GUI plan you can send out it as a python code from where you can start your python programming.

I know numerous things here would have bobbed over your head, yet it is beyond the realm of imagination to expect to disclose how to utilize the Qt4 library in a solitary instructional exercise. You can allude to sentdex PyQt4 instructional exercise arrangement to know more on the best way to utilize PyQt4 and Qt originator programming.

Python Program for Raspberry Pi Speaking Alarm Clock

The total python code for this task is given toward the finish of this page. You can legitimately run it on your Raspberry pi to get yield, yet further underneath I have clarified the program into little bits with the goal that you can see how the program functions.

Practically 50% of the code is as of now composed for us by the Qt fashioner programming, this code has then data about the sort, style, estimate and position of the articles that are over our screen. Presently all that we need to do is give reason and capacity to these articles.

The 7-portion show is utilized to show the present time. The set-time object is utilized to choose the alert time and the catch "set caution" ought to be clicked to set the alert on the chose time. The content line at the base shows when the alert is set and other helpful data. Aside from that we additionally need to play voice alert when the caution is set and activated.

For our program we need the PyQt4 for structuring the GUI and espeak to play voice alert and time bundle strftime to peruse the present time from Pi. So we import all the three bundles utilizing the beneath line of code.

```
from PyQt4 import QtCore, QtGui #PyQt4
```

is used for designing the GUI

from espeak import espeak #text to speech sonversion

from time import strftime # To get time from Raspberry pi

Next we have a piece a codes which was acquired from the Qt creator, these codes will comprise of the position and size of the gadgets that we have put on the screen. We have altered the code a little to dole out reason to the gadget. First on the 7-portion LCD gadget we need to show the present time, this should be possible by utilizing the strftime technique which will give us the present time that is running on Pi. We would then be able to show this time on the LCD as demonstrated as follows.

```
self.Time_LCD = QtGui.QLCDNumber(self.
centralwidget)

self.Time_LCD.setObjectName(_fromUt-
f8("Time_LCD"))
```

```
self.Time_LCD.setDigitCount(8)

self.Time_LCD.display(strf-
time("%H"+":"+"%M"+":"+"%S")) #get time
from Pi and display it

self.gridLayout.addWidget(self.
Time_LCD, 1, 0, 1, 3)
```

Next we have a catch squeezed button, when this catch is squeezed we need to set the caution. So we utilize a technique called button_pressed. At whatever point this catch is squeezed the capacity button_pressed will be called.

```
self.pushButton    =    QtGui.QPushButton(
self.centralwidget)

    self.pushButton.setObjectName(_fromUt-
f8("pushButton"))

    self.pushButton.clicked.connect(
self.button_pressed)    #when    button
pressed call the button pressed function
```

```
    self.gridLayout.addWidget(self.pushBut-
ton, 2, 1, 1, 1)

    MainWindow.setCentralWidget(self.
centralwidget)
```

The button_pressed work is demonstrated as follows. Here we read the estimations of hour and minutes from the set time gadget. This data will be in type of string, so it tends to be cut to get the estimation of hour and minutes and put away in the variable alarm_h and alarm_m. When we have the estimation of moment and hour we can utilize this to contrast it and current minutes and hour.

At last after the set time is perused we likewise show a book utilizing the string variable message. This message will be shown as a mark content.

```
def button_pressed(self): #when set alarm
button is pressed

    print("Button Pressed")
```

```
    alarm_time = str(self.Set_Time.time())

    self.alarm_h = int(alarm_time[19:21])
#value of hour is sotred in index value 19
and 20

    self.alarm_m = int (alarm_time[23:25])
#value of minute is sotred in index value 23
and 24

    message = "Alarm is set at " +
str(self.alarm_h) + " hours " + str(
self.alarm_m) + " minutes"

    self.label.setText(_translate("Main-
Window", message, None)) #display the
message on GUI screen

    espeak.synth (message) #speak the
message through audio jack
```

We likewise give a voice alert expressing
that the caution was set for someone or
other time by utilizing the espeak technique. This strategy just talks any content
went to it by means of the sound jack. Here
the string in the variable message is per-

used out

```
espeak.synth (message) #speak the message through audio jack
```

At long last we need one more strategy, that contrasts the present time and set time and when both match it needs to inform the client through discourse. For this reason we have the opportunity work in our code, it contrasts the current_h and alarm_h and current_m with alarm_m. At the point when both match it triggers the alert by talking the content put away in the variable message1. You can modify the variable message1 in the event that you wish to cause the clock to talk something different; at the present time it will wish you great morning alongside the present time and day.

```
def Time(self): #Function to compare current time with set time

    self.Time_LCD.display(strf-
```

```python
time("%H"+":"+"%M"+":"+"%S"))

    self.current_h = int (strftime("%H"))

    self.current_m = int (strftime("%M"))

    if (self.current_h == self.alarm_h)
and (self.current_m == self.alarm_m) and
((int(strftime("%S"))%15) == 0): #if the
both time match

        print("ALARM ON!!!!!")

        message1 = " The time is " + str(
self.alarm_h) + " : " + str(self.alarm_m) + "
on " + strftime("%A")

        message = "Sir, Good morning.. This
is your wake up Alarm." + message1

        self.label.setText(_translate("Main-
Window",message1, None)) #display the
message on GUI screen

        espeak.synth (message) #speak the
message through audio jack
```

time.sleep(1)

Hardware Set-up for Raspberry Pi Alarm Clock

The Hardware set-up for this task is entirely basic. We are utilizing simply utilizing a 3.5" TFT LCD screen with our PI. To set up the showcase you can pursue the Interfacing Pi with 3.5" LCD instructional exercise. When your interfacing is finished you ought to have the option to utilize the stylus and explore through the OS of raspberry pi. So as to play the sound you have to have a speaker, I have associated by versatile speaker to pi through AUX link. Once everything is set and the program is propelled my set-up resembled this underneath.

Working of Pi based Speaking Alarm Clock

Set up the equipment as appeared above and afterward ensure you have introduced PyQt4 and Espeak on your Pi. At that point utilize then python code given underneath, simply glue it in the python IDLE and run the program. It will dispatch the GUI window as demonstrated as follows

It shows the present time and furthermore gives a book box to set the alert. Utilize your stylus to set the caution time and push on set alert catch. This will give you a voice message expressing that the caution is set. Presently simply hold up till the present time appeared on the 7-seg show is equivalent to the caution time. At the point when its equivalent the alert is set off, this will again give a voice message with current time and day. This alert will rehash multiple times before the moment esteem changes.

This is only a base for the undertaking and you can without quite a bit of a stretch expand over by including rest and stop button. Likewise, redo the voice message dependent on your inclination or dependent on area and so forth?

Code

Speaking alarm clock using Raspberry Pi
#Connect 3.5" LCD and speaker though AUX and run the program with PyQt4 and espeak packages

GUI code was created using Qt Designer

```
import sys
import time
from PyQt4 import QtCore, QtGui #PyQt4 is used for designing the GUI
from espeak import espeak #text to speech sonversion
from time import strftime # To get time from Raspberry pi
#Code from Qt Designer
try:
    _fromUtf8 = QtCore.QString.fromUtf8
except AttributeError:
    def _fromUtf8(s):
        return s
```

```
try:
    _encoding = QtGui.QApplication.Uni-
codeUTF8
    def _translate(context, text, disambig):
        return QtGui.QApplication.translate(con-
text, text, disambig, _encoding)
except AttributeError:
    def _translate(context, text, disambig):
        return QtGui.QApplication.translate(con-
text, text, disambig)
class Ui_MainWindow(object):
    def setupUi(self, MainWindow):
        self.alarm_h = 0
        self.alarm_m = 0


        MainWindow.setObjectName(_fromUtf8("
MainWindow"))
        MainWindow.resize(676, 439)


        self.centralwidget = QtGui.QWidget(
MainWindow)
        self.centralwidget.setObjectName(_from-
Utf8("centralwidget"))
        self.gridLayout = QtGui.QGridLayout(self.
centralwidget)
        self.gridLayout.setObjectName(_fromUt-
```

```
f8("gridLayout"))
        self.label = QtGui.QLabel(self.central-
widget)


    font = QtGui.QFont()
    font.setPointSize(14)
    self.label.setFont(font)
        self.label.setObjectName(_fromUtf8("la-
bel"))
    self.gridLayout.addWidget(self.label, 3, 0,
1, 1)


    self.Time_LCD    =    QtGui.QLCDNumber(
self.centralwidget)
    self.Time_LCD.setObjectName(_fromUtf8("
Time_LCD"))
    self.Time_LCD.setDigitCount(8)
                self.Time_LCD.display(strf-
time("%H"+":"+"%M"+":"+"%S"))   #get   time
from Pi and display it
    self.gridLayout.addWidget(self.Time_LCD,
1, 0, 1, 3)
    self.timer = QtCore.QTimer(MainWindow)
    self.timer.timeout.connect(self.Time)
    self.timer.start(1000)
```

```python
    current_time = QtCore.QTime()
    self.Set_Time = QtGui.QTimeEdit(self.centralwidget)
    self.Set_Time.setObjectName(_fromUtf8("Set_Time"))
        self.Set_Time.setTime(current_time.currentTime())
    self.gridLayout.addWidget(self.Set_Time, 2, 0, 1, 1)


    self.pushButton = QtGui.QPushButton(self.centralwidget)
    self.pushButton.setObjectName(_fromUtf8("pushButton"))
            self.pushButton.clicked.connect(self.button_pressed)
    self.gridLayout.addWidget(self.pushButton, 2, 1, 1, 1)
    MainWindow.setCentralWidget(self.centralwidget)


    self.menubar = QtGui.QMenuBar(MainWindow)
            self.menubar.setGeometry(QtCore.QRect(0, 0, 676, 21))
```

```python
        self.menubar.setObjectName(_fromUtf8("
menubar"))
        MainWindow.setMenuBar(self.menubar)


        self.statusbar = QtGui.QStatusBar(Main-
Window)
        self.statusbar.setObjectName(_fromUt-
f8("statusbar"))
        MainWindow.setStatusBar(self.statusbar)
        self.retranslateUi(MainWindow)
        QtCore.QMetaObject.connectSlotsBy-
Name(MainWindow)
#End of code from Qt Designer

    def retranslateUi(self, MainWindow): #up-
date the GUI window
    print("Dispay Re-translated")
        MainWindow.setWindowTitle(_trans-
late("MainWindow", "MainWindow", None))
        self.label.setText(_translate("MainWin-
dow", "Alarm curretly Turned off", None))
    self.pushButton.setText(_translate("Main-
Window", "Set Alarm", None))


    def Time(self): #Function to compare cur-
```

rent time with set time

```
            self.Time_LCD.display(strf-
time("%H"+":"+"%M"+":"+"%S"))
    self.current_h = int (strftime("%H"))
    self.current_m = int (strftime("%M"))
        if (self.current_h == self.alarm_h)
and (self.current_m == self.alarm_m) and
((int(strftime("%S"))%15) == 0): #if the both
time match
        print("ALARM ON!!!!!")


        message1 = " The time is " + str(
self.alarm_h) + " : " + str(self.alarm_m) + " on "
+ strftime("%A")
        message = "Sir, Good morning.. This is
your wake up Alarm." + message1


        self.label.setText(_translate("MainWin-
dow",message1, None)) #display the message
on GUI screen
        espeak.synth (message) #speak the mes-
sage through audio jack
        time.sleep(1)
```

```python
    def button_pressed(self): #when set alarm
button is pressed
        print("Button Pressed")
        alarm_time = str(self.Set_Time.time())


        self.alarm_h   =   int(alarm_time[19:21])
#value of hour is sotred in index value 19 and
20
        self.alarm_m = int (alarm_time[23:25])
#value of minute is sotred in index value 23
and 24
        message = "Alarm is set at " + str(
self.alarm_h) + " hours " + str(self.alarm_m) + "
minutes"
        self.label.setText(_translate("MainWin-
dow", message, None)) #display the message
on GUI screen
        espeak.synth (message) #speak the mes-
sage through audio jack
if __name__ == "__main__": #main function


    app = QtGui.QApplication(sys.argv)
    MainWindow = QtGui.QMainWindow()
    ui = Ui_MainWindow()
    ui.setupUi(MainWindow)
    MainWindow.show()
```

```
sys.exit(app.exec_())
```

Thank

You !!!